DEDICATED TO *Gary Gene Crowell*

This book is in loving memory of my bearded stepfather, who passed away in 1998 from diabetes. The good ones always die young.

Is it possible...

to comment on the current state of fashion, culture, and the economy through the careful observation of men's beards? I was on a mission to find out, but also to do something I thought might amuse an audience as well as myself. Using San Francisco as my main study area, I took to the city's streets in search of beards on faces of people, animals, or inanimate objects. In essence, this is a social study, an art project, and a unique record of a moment in time in a particular place.

I loved /hated the unpredictable result of asking a stranger, "Um, excuse me, can I take your picture?" What a nightmare. I was fortunate enough to have several friends and peers who wanted to do a little hunting to add to the collection as well.

I hope you all enjoy the uncomfortable reality of this socially awkward task I took on, and my ridiculous commentary that goes with it. Have a laugh, and may you be inspired to go out and make an ass of yourself in the name of a personal goal or project!

Text, photography, and design:
Juliann Brown

Contributing photographers:
Kevin Bergthold, Jessica Bergthold, Chiaki Hachisu, Jason Wilkey, Kelly Puleio, Alexandra Kirby, Angela Vinci

Copy editor:
Adam E. Stone

ISBN #: 978-0615603445

Special thanks to:

Jason Carter, Christina Empedocles, Jennifer Strand, Jason Martinez, Kristi Beddow, Nate Van Dyke, Nancy Crowell, Sam McCowen, Hobart Beasley, Gary Beasley, Rosenell Beasley, Summer Koide, Sushant Kamath, Devon Chulick, Livia Ching, Matt Gerring, Matt Vigeland, Joanne Carter, James Carter, Julian Carter, Rocky, Tom Price, Dan Mallory, David Bergthold, Kevin Bergthold, Jessica Bergthold, Chiaki Hachisu, Richie Ditta, Alex Pierce, Alex Wojciechowski, Sarah Ditzer, Keith Handelsman, Boni Uzilevsky, Ryan McCaffrey, Paige Brown, Charlie and Nadeem, Kai, Zach, D-Structure, Mad Dog in the Fog, and everyone who participated to help make this happen.

Extra special thanks to:

Adam E. Stone for being an amazing mentor on so many levels throughout this project.

The Beard Hunter Copyright © 2012 by Juliann Brown.
All rights reserved. Printed in the United States of America. No part of this book may be reproduced or transmitted in any form or by any means, electronic or mechanical, including photocopying, recording, or by an information storage and retrieval system-except by a reviewer who may quote brief passages in a review to be printed in a magazine, newspaper, or on the Web-without permission in writing from Jbear Publishing.

For more information, contact JBear Publishing.
Email: juliannbrown@me.com

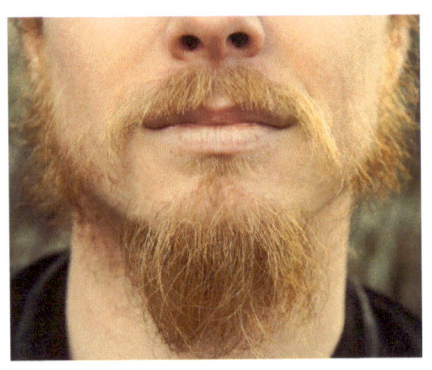

BROWN BAG *Bandits*

Met my first three bearded beauties in one neat little package. I found them in a small coastal town in Northern California. We were escaping the city for the day, and right as we were parking I spotted a bearded cowboy riding by on a horse. We later found the horse tied up outside a little saloon. She doesn't have a beard but her owner did, but he got away before I could get to him. She's just here because I never got my pony as a kid.

   Right across the street there were three good 'ole boys, hanging out and having an afternoon 40. They thought I was C.I.A. at first and tried to run, but quickly came around with a little bit of gab. My better half was with me and he can talk the hind leg off a horse, or I would have probably given up. We heard some crazy stories from these three. I'd tell you, but then they'd have to kill me.

Missing hind leg due to my husband talking it off.

A FULL Fourth

I forced my husband, Jack, and our dog, Kai, out with me today on my hunt. We put our camo on and went via automobile. It was the 4th of July, so I was thinking I could find some super-patriotic, half-naked person walking around town, as they do here. Sadly, the crazy folks weren't out yet. It all worked out in the end, because when I saw this bear, I knew I had found my beard. In seconds I went from granny-driving to Mario Andretti, whipping around three blocks, skidding into a parking spot, and kicking Jack out to run and catch these two for me while I grabbed my camera: "Go, Go, GO!"

With this we got Patrick: nice and full, multi-colored arrangement with a fabulous accessory called Lisa on his arm.

Patrick's shirt is from a famous "Bear" tavern in our fine city. Many out-of-town straight bikers have gone in there not knowing the men are bikers (bears) who like other male bikers.

I can't think of a better time to be a fly on the wall.

FacToid: I have sunglasses just like Lisa's.

Redhead/beard counT: 01

Oranjegekte

(FacToid: OranjegekTe means orange mania)

So I was headed down Haight Street when this giant, 6'5" guy burst out of a bar onto the street with a large entourage of cheering people in tow. He was so covered in orange that he seemed to have the fire trail of a comet. Even his truck was orange! The World Cup game between the Netherlands and Uruguay had just ended (3-2, Netherlands). It's safe to say he was a Netherlands fan. I wasn't shy with this photo at all, as I was one of at least a dozen people literally stopping traffic for a snapshot. They were all yelling some nonsense, "Hup Holland! Hup"! I am not a sports enthusiast, but you didn't have to be to appreciate the moment.

    He looks like Hulk Hogan. Is he? No? Maybe? I can't tell if he's bald or not with that hat on. Brother Hogan?

I do NOT have sunglasses like his. Lisa and I are jealous.

Bark AT THE MOON

My friend Tom and I got together for lunch (drinks) and I mentioned to him that I had to find my beard while we were out, and then it hit me like a frying pan in the face that at that very moment I was sitting next to Wolverine's brother from another mother. When I asked him if he would be my subject, he said, "Sorry, no photos of me, but you can photograph my driver's license". How could I say no to that?

What WOULD TOPHER DO?

Believe it or not, I have to do other things besides gallivant around the city taking photos of beards. I still have bills to pay. While out for a meeting today, I ran into this guy. For a moment I wondered if I was meeting Jesus himself, but it turns out his name was Topher.

I hope you enjoy the little wispy hair bits sticking up on the top of his head as much as I did. It wasn't even windy out.

SOLID AS A
Rocky

Behold Rocky. If you can make the magic happen with your beard grooming like this one, don't hesitate to contact me for the sequel. What I love about this picture most is that he's looking out over the Mission District, which is the predominately Hispanic area of San Francisco.

I should have taken his photo in front of one of the famous murals in the neighborhood, but I felt his amazing clipper wizardry needed to stand on its own.

Please relax and enjoy the lovely view of power lines in front of our apartment.

Smoking LOTUS

What happens when you go to the art store? Good things. Great tools for creating surrounded by lots of savory characters buying them.

It probably goes without saying, but this was a good day of hunting. You gotta love San Francisco's air of "be yourself." I'm wondering if this is the guy who brought back plaid shirts? I went and bought one immediately.

"Samedi's Cookbook" by Thee HypnoTics was The song playing while I worked on This. PerfecT. If you haven'T heard iT yet, listen To iT now!

The Guy Who Needs No-dozer

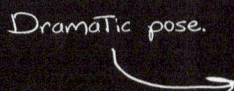

Dramatic pose.

BAND OF BEARDED
Brothers

I found myself back at the bar Mad Dog again. It's easier to find prey after a glass of courage, and that's a great area for hunting. These guys were more than eager to be my beard models.

I spotted the guy in the middle first, then he quickly recruited the other two ... then the fourth. They seemed to be good friends, but all had very different personalities, as you can clearly see. From left to right, we have the poser, the soldier, and he-who-needs-no-dozer. Guy smiley, the fourth guy, joined in later.

I love these guys for making my mission so easy that day. They were a perfect sitcom cast. We'll call it "The Odd Quadruple." A soap opera will pick up the guy on the left, Devon, at some point. He has more than proven his skills.

Redhead/beard count: 02

$\mathcal{E}$=MC²

He wouldn't tell me his name, but I really wanted to call him Mr. Einstein. When I tried to ask the little guy (he had to be under 5' tall) about the theory of relativity, he completely ignored me, focusing instead on trying to tie his beard into a ponytail with a rubber band larger than his head. I suppose we all want to look our very best, especially if we are going to be featured in a book about beards, but I preferred him sans rubber band.

No hairspray was harmed in the shooting of this beard.

Horny JACK

It turns out there was prey in my own home: my other half, Jack. If you're wondering if he's a Satyr (half man, half goat) he's not. Bestiality is not my thing. I caught him as he shaved, and he just happened to be standing a few feet in front of a bull skull we have hanging up on our bathroom wall.

After his shave, I served him his favorite dinner, a nice tin can and some shrubbery.

Taken just before horns sprouted and moustache fell off.

Time for a new wife-beater.

Redhead/beard count: 03

"Festive holiday moustaches are hard to grow" beard.

"Jingling the bells" beard.

"Fu Manchu hybrid" beard.

"He works hard for the money" beard.

"Bromance" beard.

"My brows go red when I'm angry" beard.

"Shit floats" beard.

"Slap happy" beard.

"Aren't I adorable?" beard.

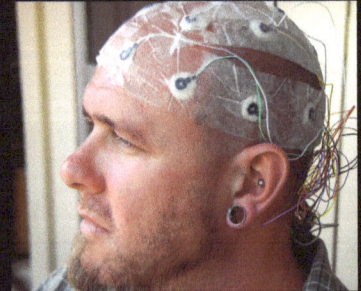
"Tech head" beard.

"King of a one bedroom castle" beard.

"I ♥ Mexico" beard.

Jack
OVERLOAD

My collection of photos of Jack's face from over the years is staggering, so I couldn't resist giving you a little dose of what I have to put up with on a daily basis.

Throughout all our years together, I've never seen my husband without facial hair. I call his beard a prosthetic chin. He shaved just the chin portion off once to achieve a good Fu Manchu and it looked a little like his face caved in. I haven't encouraged him to shave it off since.

"The yolk's on you" beard.

WON'T YOU TAKE ME TO
Smoky Town?

It only took me three months to drop off a borrowed external hard drive at my old office. When doing so, I had the opportunity to hunt for a "friend beard." This is Smoky Town Dan. He enjoys heavy metal, cigarettes, Motorhead tattoos, vans, and long walks on the beach.

    I loved my prey that day not only because of the smoke rolling out of his nose, but because his reflection in the building showed signs of a six pack and a steak the night before, no doubt consumed while listening to Megadeath. The camera never lies.

← Some ironic T-shirt artwork for everyone to enjoy.

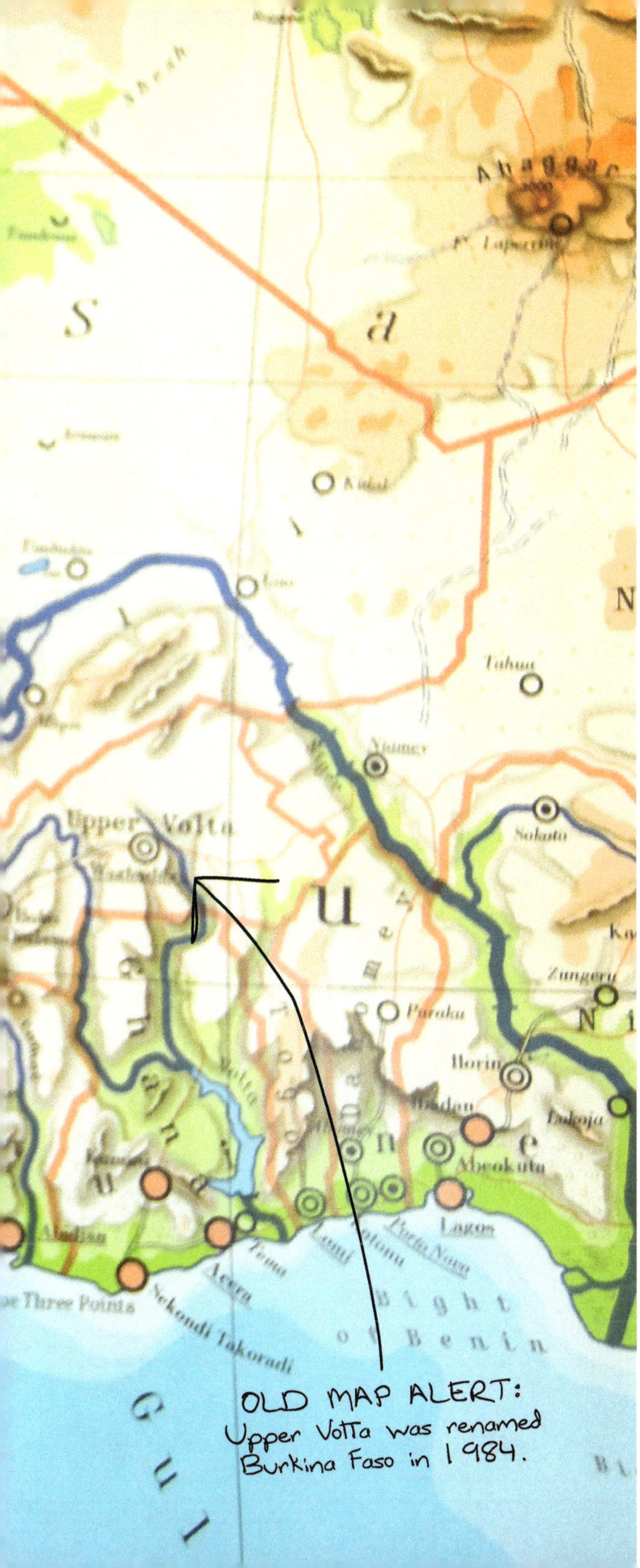

OLD MAP ALERT: Upper Volta was renamed Burkina Faso in 1984.

YIN AND *Yang*

My friend Jason kept complaining about his itchy beard, and I knew he wanted to shave it, so I had to get involved before the opportunity was lost.

    I knocked on his door. He opened it. I jabbed him in the neck with a tranquilizer dart, hogtied him, and shaved his beard off only half way. Call me committed. A sexy story, yes, but I'm sure you're shocked to hear it's not true. He did, however, let me talk him into keeping his new beard-do for almost a day.

    As you can see below, my husband looks a little too excited to play barber, but Jason let him do it anyway.

"I wanna be a barber when I grow up."

Here's Dave holding his portrait. Last year his wife, Laurie, and sister in-law, Jessica, saw a goat they thought looked like Dave, so Jessica and Dave's brother, Kevin, surprised him with a custom caricature they had a friend paint. I get it. →

photo by Kevin Bergthold

I'M NOT AS Think AS YOU DRUNK I AM

This is what happens when you give your friends, in this case my friend Dave, Big Daddy beer. If you're a beer drinker, but are unaccustomed to the power of this strong ale, be warned people. Four beers will put you in a place that usually requires twice that amount.

That said, the photo and I distort to some degree: Dave wasn't destroyed, just not enjoying my camera flash. The four-beer-rule didn't kick in until a few hours later.

Redhead/beard count: 04

Stephen King's "Christine" can't touch this car.

ART CAR Eddie

Eddie bought me a Maker's Mark before our photo shoot, so I was able to get a bit more info than I normally would from my hunted.

Turns out he owned this crazy-looking art car that was often parked by our house. The car was eventually impounded, and he decided to let it go, so I was pretty happy I had already taken photos of it: so I can show you guys the madness on four wheels. When he told me he'd spent 10 years collecting the items on the car, I envisioned his place being on an episode of the TV show *Hoarders* before his art car assembly. Let's just hope for his sake he has a garage.

Cheers my free-bird friend. Our photo session was one of my favorites.

Have you hugged your heart today?

Redhead/beard count: 05

"Please get all your shit off of me."

Eddie exposed his infatuation with shoes.

These dreads deserve an honorable mention. — They could easily be a beard, or two, of their own.

↳ The sTore's bouncer.

ArTisTs' "blue lighT special" pile.

The herd is coming.

They all drank The Kool-A

HAPPY
Trailers
TO YOU.

On a jaunt to Colorado, I began to feel as if the tables had turned, and couldn't help but wonder who was the hunter and who the hunted. Not to mention the trouble I had spotting this smiling, bearded man with

SALT and JEFFER

I wish you could see the back of this guy's hair. It's cut straight across like his beard. I first spotted him from the back and thought, "Oh look, another old guy with a big beard," but to my surprise and delight he was probably only in his mid to late thirties. His name is Jeff, but I'd like to rename him "Salt-N-Jeffer." Let's just call him the proper seasoning for any occasion.

← FacToid: The bob haircut was invented in the 1920s. Jeff brings it back in beard form.

I want that bike. →

PRECITA *Palace* PORCH PEOPLE

There is no shortage of socializing with the tenants of my building, which we like to refer to as "Precita Palace." We are all around the same age and pretty much at the same point in life. This means stressed-out, over-worked, and underpaid, so it's very common for a "party on the porch" to take place where we all unwind. Think of it as a modern day speakeasy without a door fee.

My capture, Alex, is one of my eight palace people. He's probably looking at me like that because he knows how badly I want to steal his hat.

FacToid: AbsinThe occupied This drink mixer unTil just before The photo was Taken.

We don't mess around when winding down.

YOU WANT *Huh?*

Here is my deer in headlights. That face is full of "HUH?"
This old guy knew I was taking his picture, so it wasn't really a surprise, I'm just not sure it all sunk in immediately.

It went kind of like this...

Me: Hello, sir. I'm doing a photo journal on beards and I would love to include you in it. Can I take a picture of you?
Him: Huh? Okay.

Me: Can you please sign a photo release so that I can use your photo in print?
Him: Huh? I'll take cash.

Me: Is $5.00 okay?
Him: (grabs it)

Me: I'll just get a few photos and then you're good to go.
Him: Huh? Okay.

I took two photos then he turned and started to walk away.

Me: Thank you, sir.
Him: Huh? I'm going to get smokes.

I think I just found Medusa's long lost son.

Redhead/beard count: 06

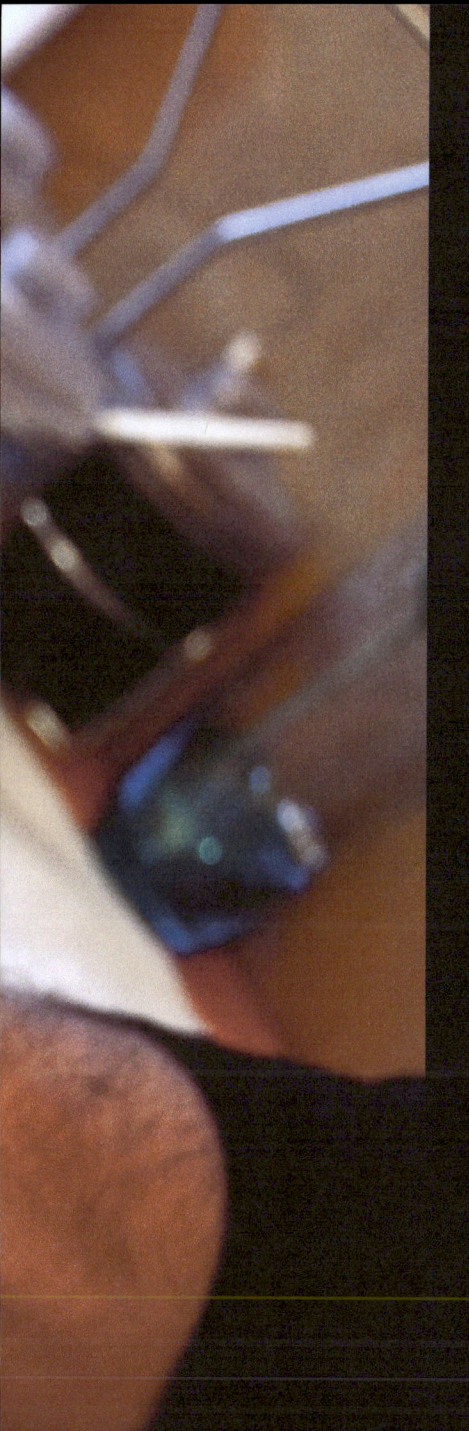

← Beard in progress.

MAGIC Munkee

This is my friend Nate Van Dyke. I call him Munkee. Since it's illegal to hunt monkeys, and his stubble wasn't quite enough, he decided to draw a beard for me on one of those paper tablecloths during dinner.

The swirl around the eye, and the hanging tongue, might represent alcohol consumption from earlier; however, a feeling of confusion and general annoyance is pretty normal for both of us, so it could just be representing the mood of the day.

Munkee helped me get my very first beard photo, so I have to give him a lot of credit for helping me get this damn thing going. Thank you my dear friend :)

Strange collaborative drawing made during dinner. →

← Temporary fill-in beard.

STALKING Mr. Fu

By the time I came upon this victim, I was constantly scanning for beards. My friends were on the lookout as well. I had already had many lost beard-tunities, and I almost lost Mr. Fu. I spotted him from a distance as my dogs did their business at the park. After they finished, I ran toward him like a crazy lady, catching him just as he was getting into his car. I'm lucky he didn't pepper spray me.

I asked him where the name "Mr. Fu" came from, and this is what he told me ...

"Back in the day, a friend gave me the nickname Fu Man Jew. Whenever I went to my neighborhood bar, when I walked in, a group would yell, 'Hey, it's Fu Man Jew.' Doug, an old Chinese gentleman, felt that this greeting was insulting to me. After a few months, I walked in one day and before anyone else could react, Doug yelled out, 'Mr. Fu, how are you?' and Mr. Fu stuck."

I also found out he's a wine vendor and a painter. I always support wine and art, since they go so well together. The picture to the right is Mr. Fu's first painting, sold in the late 90s. He's been rockin' the facial hair in a good way for a long time now. A black belt in beards, you might say.

FacToid: First painting Mr. Fu sold in The late 90s. I'm guessing This look caused The birth of his nickname.

Some of Mr. Fu's painTings...

Kelly Puleio took this
photo of Mr. Fu.
I love it. It made me
kick myself for not
doing more
night hunting.

More of Mr. Fu's paintings...

photo by Kelly Puleio

Warning: Do noT iron imporTanT cloThing iTems on This ironing board.

Love HAIGHT

I really needed help recovering from a string of bad hunting experiences, including on Haight Street. Luckily, I was still on Haight when I found "Not on Crack, Jack." He was sitting on the ground working on his own art project, so he was happy to be a part of mine.

    I wanted to ask him if I could wax the tips of his moustache, because it's so handlebar-worthy, but talked myself out of it … since I didn't have any wax on me. That would just be weird.

    Thanks for the mental Band-Aid Jack, and keep saying "no" to crack.

Geek noTe: My friend poinTed ouT ThaT This guy looks like Boromir from "Lord of The Rings." Agreed.

Redhead/beard counT: 07

Convict dance sequence Time...

Does your momma know you wear That hat?

Keeks The Broad Beard School of Hip Hop is Temporarily closed for "remodeling."

Broad BEARD

Bounty hunting was the name of the game with this beauty. With two counts of indecent exposure, four counts of smoking weed in public, and one count of assault on a neighbor, we picked up Keeks the Broad Beard and booked her.

Many convicts don't know how to cope in the outside world and find solace on the "inside." You can see this is definitely the case for Keeks by the happy dance she did when we tried to get her mug shot. To calm her down we gave her a cigarette, ripped her hat off, and told her we would auction off her hog if she didn't chill.

Urban scripture. It'll have to do for now.

SEND ME AN Angel

This may have been the nicest human being I've ever met. His name is Gerard (or Gerry, if you prefer) from Northern Ireland. He was oozing a beautiful energy that was so thick I almost slipped on some of it when I was talking to him. He had extraordinary "hug me" powers to the point where I had to mentally pry myself away.

Gerry quietly slipped away through some pearly gates covered with street dust to his apartment after we were done talking.

HOW You DOIN'?

This is Ben, with his crazy-white, perfectly-straight teeth. "Whack Grill" will never be one of his nicknames. He's probably one of those people who brushes and flosses after every meal, and still sleeps with his retainer. I really had to restrain myself from adding a twinkle to his teeth in this photo. Really.

We didn't talk about anything at all. There was no need. Not sure I could have anyway.

ATTA Boy

This was the happiest guy I encountered on my hunts. He didn't speak a single word to me. Just smiled, nodded, and did a little jig every time I spoke to him. He had great energy. There are a lot of retreats out there where the participants don't speak for a number of days. Maybe he was doing that on his own accord, or had a bet with a friend. Sometimes we all just need to shut the hell up anyway.

Redhead/beard count: 08

Note: multifunctional hoodie may also be used as a napkin.

ALL IN THE
Family

Too nice to be as scary as me.

I went hunting with (for) family. This is my sister-in-law, Jo, and brother-in-law, James. They came over the pond from England for a visit, and we stayed at the same house that my husband and I had rented for a weekend before, where we took the photo of ourselves to the immediate right. I wanted Jo and James to replicate it, but she's far too nice to capture the madness I can naturally display.

Jo had all of her belongings urinated on by our newly adopted dog, Zach, but she ended up loving him so much she has repeatedly asked me to bring a vial of his pee over to her in the UK when we go. He got a little poop on her boob too, but for some reason she only wants the pee.

Me and my daily prey.

Little pee machine.

FacToid: We are all members of "The Giant Sunglass Club."

JAMIE HYNEMAN'S
Twin
IS MY FRIEND

Alex isn't really related to Jamie Hyneman from *MythBusters*, but the resemblance is obvious. Alex, however, will not be putting any cannonballs through your walls.

I asked him to bring some of his hats, since he usually has one on when I see him, and he brought like five of them so we had no problem with variety. The guy knows how to rock the hat.

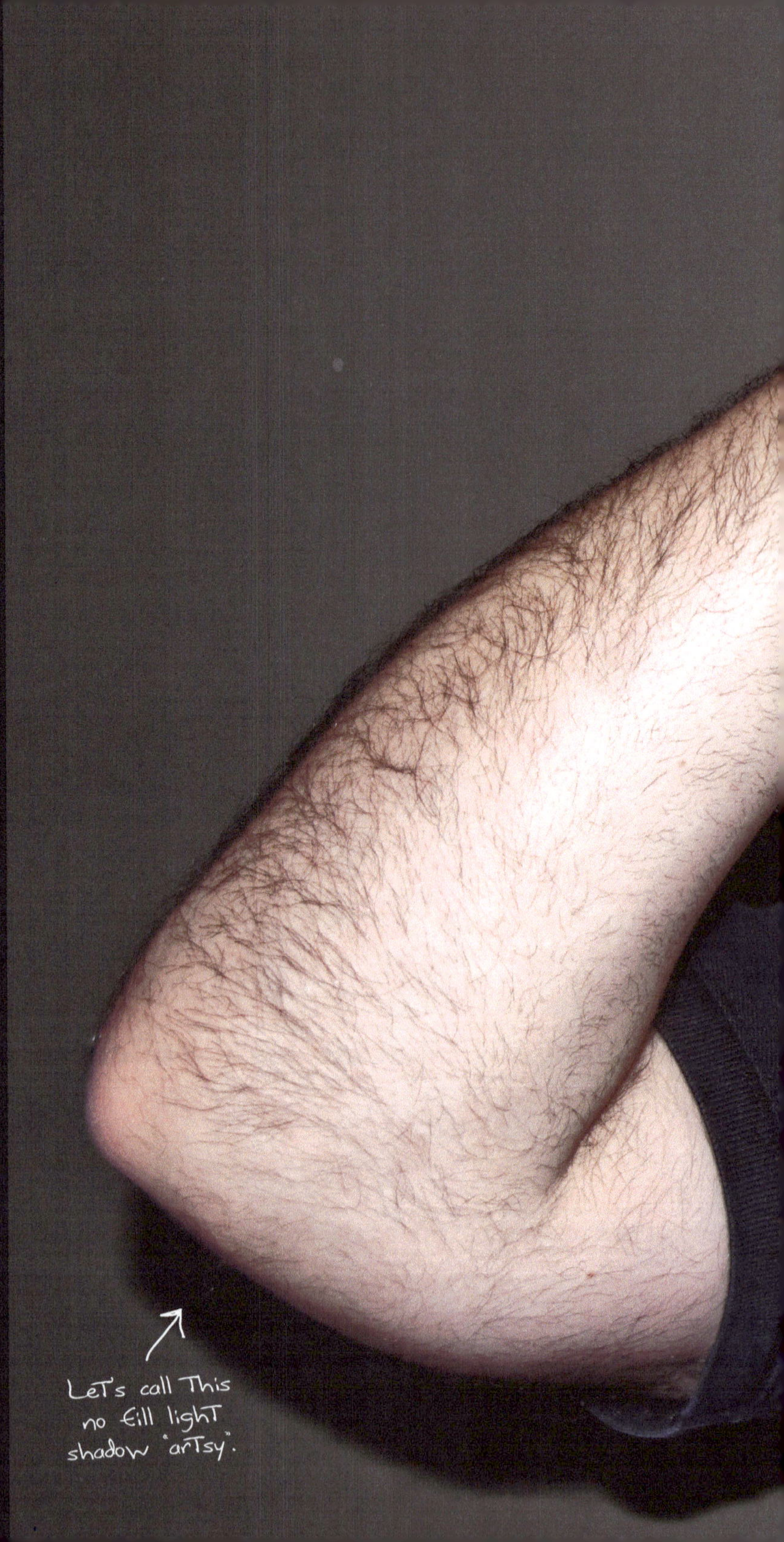

Let's call This no fill light shadow "arTsy".

The face might suggest constipation but he's just trying to loosen a bolt.

Cycle SURGEON

While walking around with a breakfast burrito baby, I found Cycle Surgeon Dan at his Courier Care Unit. We went into his shop that day for bike reasons, and he turned my day around. Just an hour before, I had been turned down by some random douche outside of a pet store. Ass. Rejection makes it harder to ask the next person, so I owe Dr. Dan a big "thanks" for keeping me going with this project.

I wonder if he stashes some of his small hardware in his beard. There's plenty of room and he's running out of it in his shop.

Redhead/beard count: 09

CAPTAIN *Toad*

Oh, the Embarcadero, the land of tourists, silver men, fishy smells, and Mr. Toads.

    This is one of the tour bus drivers in the Wharf area of San Francisco. He looks like a damn good captain, if you ask me.

    He let me stop him mid-sentence to pose for a photo while he was delivering his script to his captivated Midwestern audience and their cousins/wives. Someone give this man a raise.

Laser beam eyes.

Yoga BEAR

I had no idea I would be hunting bears on this day, and I didn't want to disturb this one doing yoga in the park, but he wasn't my normal sort of bearded victim.

As I stood about five feet away and was getting my camera out, I looked down and noticed my dog, Kai, had another dog's ball in her mouth. Next to her was another dog, accompanied by its angry owner with an empty ball tosser. The next fifteen minutes were spent anxiously trying to get the ball out of Kai's mouth, while the other dog and its owner stared holes in me. All while we were in the yoga bear's Zen space. I was covered in slobber from the battle. That dog loves balls and this guy probably hates me.

I'm wondering why this guy likes birds so much. Was he once a beatnik bear? His bird tattoos don't look all that old. Maybe he's hoping they'll help him float away when he meditates. That was clearly not going to happen today with all the commotion surrounding him. Dragon tattoos would have been more appropriate for the occasion.

Bear Toes go Through a lot.

← David Bowie "Ziggy Stardust" T-shirt that brings a slight feeling of jealousy.

No matter how many times I see people with ear tunnels (husband included) they still make my earlobes hurt.

Nice PANTS

Jose was here from Germany visiting my neighbor. If it weren't for working from home, my eyes would never have had the joy of his fashion frenzy. His salt and pepper stubble was plenty o' beard after evaluating the whole package. Nice shirt. Nice cherry blossoms. FABULOUS PANTS. I can't compete with his ensemble so I'm taking Germany off my "Places To Go" list due to lack of proper attire.

THE *Flavor* SAVER

I'm not a hiker, but I went on one. I have no idea where we were, but it was nice. At the top of a hill I decided my hiking friend, Keith, qualified to be one of my victims. It's not a giant beard, but hair below the lip is more commonly known as "The Flavor Saver" which is worth a mention. Flavors to save are of many varieties, but most of your minds went straight to the gutter, as well they should have.

There I am in someone's sunglass reflection again. Go figure.

Banana slug I almost stepped on during the hike. No beard, but worthy.

Odd Factoid: The Banana slug is the UC Santa Cruz mascot. Seriously.

HIGH AS A *Kai*

Say hello to one of my babies, Kai. This is what you would look like if you were captured stoned and eating ice cream, or if you had just been woken up from a canine siesta. In her case, I think it was the weed.
    That's one big tongue she has. Eat your heart out Gene Simmons.

Don't get too close, she's a mouth licker and we all know where that tongue's been.

Matt
OF ALL TRADES

What do you need done? Matt can probably do it. By day, he's a sculptor, digital design wizard, office manager, ladder climber. By night, he's a screen printer, illustrator, landscaper, Capoeira Angola martial artist, beer brewer, and music mixer. In his free time, Matt likes to circle dog eggs left on his sidewalk with chalk and write "bad citizen." I'm not sure how effective it is since he lives in Oakland.

This is a "moustache optional" look.

You're drinking The wrong drink, Man.

THE Super DUDE ABIDES

As many of you would like to, I've been hunting my own family. Julian (a.k.a. Juey) is another brother-in-law; may as well be "the dude" in the movie *The Big Lebowski*. I would kill to have a photo of him in an old robe and clown pants, holding a White Russian, but for now we'll settle for a beat-up *Superman* T-shirt, drinking wine with cheesy wood paneling surrounding him.

Redhead/beard count: 10

Fuzzy DUSTY

We were at a pet store because we adopted another dog and needed pee pads. When we walked in, Dusty was there to educate us on chinchillas. Soft ... so was the chinchilla.

    In case you can't tell, the chinchilla is being held by the kid, not Dusty's chin.

Chinchilla

Chin-heaTa

Redhead/beard counT: 11

ELECTRONICS ARE MY *Bitch*

The man who looks like he has his hand in the cookie jar is Craig, your furry light and sound tech. The key to his success is the pole coming out of his head that holds up his umbrella hat. This way when it rains he can protect his equipment. The downside is his broken back, caused by always leaning over his board. You can see the pain in his eyes. Bend at the knees, Craig!

Much thanks for making the song "Tears of a Clown" stuck in my head for five days. At least it wasn't "Purple Rain." That song often causes loud outbursts of singing in public.

The "I just ripped my pants" face.

Keep your hat on David.

THEY'RE *Mine* TOO

David was working with Craig that night too, doing ... lights? Or was it also sound? Or camera? Damn. I forgot to take notes. He's smiling because unlike Craig, he bends at the knees. He was even doing a few knee bends when I took the photo. Show off.

Redhead/beard count: 12 and 13

Farmer Ted's
BROTHER FROM ANOTHER MOTHER

I would like to introduce one of Farmer Ted's other brothers, Ryan. Remember the guy who played John Cusack's ray gun wielding brother in the movie *Sixteen Candles*?

Ryan might appear to be in his natural daily gear, but I actually made him wear the props. He's always been good at taking my abuse. There's a picture of me somewhere with that damn night vision thing on too, but I will not be sharing that with you ... ever.

This is The conTinuaTion oF The shaFT.

Redhead/beard counT: 14

PLASTIC
Fantastic

While walking around my old office after taking Ryan's photo, I discovered that Snake from the videogame *Metal Gear Solid* isn't a real person, but actually a life-size man-doll. I also found out that Lara Croft isn't really Angelina Jolie … just another man-doll. Plastic surgeons are taking things way too far these days, so you can imagine my confusion at first. A few pokes later it was settled.

Don't bend over, Lara. Things will fall off or out.

Snake carries a big gun to make up for other shortcomings.

photo by Alexandra Kirby

King
FOR A MINUTE

Alexandra Kirby caught a photo of Kevin, temporary King of the Redwoods, as he waved to his subjects. Kevin doesn't look very excited, and if I were to guess why, I would say it's because whoever made his crown could have made it fit a little better. The rule is, when the crown falls off - you're no longer king. Kevin kept his on for a total of about one minute, which means he is still the longest reigning leader. All hail the king!

I LIKE Mike

Today's hunt started at Trader Joe's in San Francisco's SoMa neighborhood (I can't afford Whole Paycheck, people). Like many of us do, I shopped with an empty stomach and had nothing in my bags to snack on afterward, so I had to go buy more food from a small cafe stand right outside the market. This is where Mike with his nice, thick beard enters the story. He was peacefully eating a burrito while reading a book, so I, of course, rudely disturbed him to see if he would be my prey of the day. Of course he said yes ... I mean, look at that face. I think his mouth was still full when I shot the photo. People are so nice here ... sometimes ... almost never.

Cynical bedroom eyes can also double for McDrunky eyes. →

FacToid: Redheads look good enough in green to pull off the color combo all year without looking too Christmassy.

'Ello Matey

Does he look wasted to you? I think he was just annoyed by me. I'm pretty sure he's Australian, which usually means nice guy, but we all have our bad days. He did agree to have his photo taken, but it took some work. We left right afterward because it was too uncomfortable to stick around. I can't blame some of these people. I hate having my photo taken. Oh, the irony.

Redhead/beard count: 15

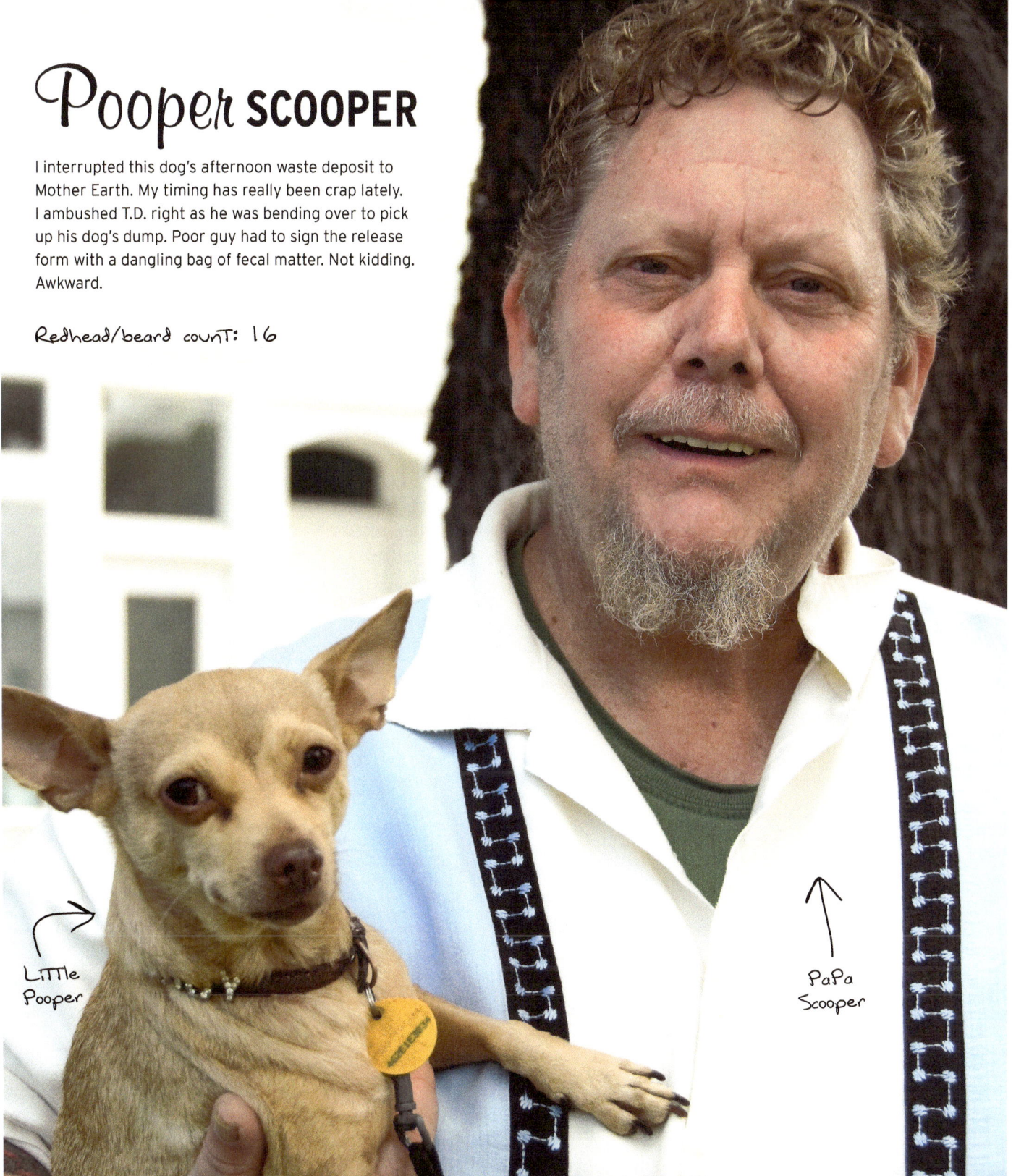

Pooper SCOOPER

I interrupted this dog's afternoon waste deposit to Mother Earth. My timing has really been crap lately. I ambushed T.D. right as he was bending over to pick up his dog's dump. Poor guy had to sign the release form with a dangling bag of fecal matter. Not kidding. Awkward.

Redhead/beard count: 16

Little Pooper

PaPa Scooper

Fast TIMES

Here we have victim Sean. I stopped him as he rode by on his bike. He was annoyed because he was in some sort of desperate hurry, but he reluctantly agreed to participate. I've been turned down enough to just roll with it, even when they're not so into having a photo taken.

Sean made me feel so rushed I didn't get the focus on his beard, but at least his curls look fabulous. He had a Euro-merican thing going on with 80s shades and a baguette in tow. He even went straight to the cafe across the street afterward. I guess he was in a hurry to get an ice cream. Savage.

He could be the offspring of Mike Damone from "Fast Times at Ridgemont High."

Damone quote time: "When it comes down to making out, whenever possible, put on side one of Led Zeppelin IV."

Some might still feel these are words to live by.

Cool lighT bulb I found at El Rio. We were noT in The red lighT disTricT.

HAVE *Another*

I hit a wall, and was so damn sick of beards I felt too stressed to find one. Instead, we decided to go for a drink without an agenda, and I ended up shooting one of Mat, the bartender. I used the "few drinks later" filter to get this lovely artist effect. Shout out to Mat at El Rio!

Woobly stool results in blurry photo effect.

That's a purdy big mic ya got There lady.

WHERE'S THE *Fire*?

I'm not sure where the fire is, but I don't think these two made it there on time with all the yelling they were doing at the pedestrians. Some of the peds were so scared they gave these two money, got in the back, and allowed the lady to yell facts at them with a microphone.

DeTachable bushes.

THE EMBARCADERO'S Bush Man

Anyone who has visited San Francisco has probably had an encounter with the Bush Man. He has hired himself to scare innocent passersby all day. He rightfully has earned a spot representing the Embarcadero's many weird tourist attractions. I wanted to scare him to flip the script, but didn't want to get smacked with a bush, so I refrained.

I'm suddenly very hungry.

Charles IN CHARGE

This is Charlie, owner of Charlie's Cafe in Bernal Heights, San Francisco. Everyone in the neighborhood knows and loves Charlie. Let's call him the "Charles in Charge" of the hood. His cafe has some good eats, a friendly, eclectic setting, and local artists' work covering the walls. Maybe someday he'll let me put some artwork up. I'm hoping a little ass kissin' by putting him in the book will help. See you soon, Charlie.

BAGEL MASTER *Brother*

Also at Charlie's Cafe, we have his brother, Nadeem. He makes bagels the way I like 'em: extra cream cheese. I had to hunt Nadeem down before he shaved his beard off, because apparently his girlfriend was begging him to get rid of it. I bet kissing him with that 'stache feels like kissing a mini bed of nails. Now that I've said that, I can only hope he doesn't drop my bagel on the floor.

Everything bagel, extra cream cheese, capers, and lox please.

Dave's stylist doubles as a chef.

← He's crazy!

Crazy DAVE

Who wears a pan for a hat? Crazy Dave, who is the inspiration for a character in the videogame *Plants vs. Zombies*. It looks like I caught him after a beard trim, but his cartoon clearly has a great face muff going on.

To switch it up, I decided to conduct a little interview for you folks ...

Me: So ... how did you become Crazy Dave?
Crazy Dave: I was the founder and general manager of PopCap Games, the San Francisco studio where the game was created.

Me: How long?
CD: From 2005-2007.

Me: Where did the pot on the head come from? Please tell me it was from a drunken moment.
CD: I'm pretty bald so I usually wear a hat outside in the summer, but the team took a few liberties ;)

Me: Do you wear a pasta strainer when it's warmer outside so you don't overheat?
CD: No, that would just give me a polka dot sunburn on my scalp.

WORLD OF Ryan-Craft

Here's a fellow designer friend, Ryan. He worked for the same company I used to work for, hence the long face. He worked on a magazine focused on a major videogame. You may have guessed which game from the title above. If you still don't know which game, you're 100% geek free and probably have no interest in *Star Trek*, Orcs, or Comic-Con.

His beard isn't crazy or anything. I'm just wondering if it goes down to his waistline. The potential is there.

Fashion observation: Undercover headphones can make one's head appear larger than it actually is.

Random space filler: This is my "Lil Goor." I drew him sometime around 1995, after being inspired by Brian Froud goblin illustrations. Back then I was crazy enough to put him on resumes I sent out. Probably not a good idea. He's finally found his place here with his lil beard :)

Spider MAN

This project is going to turn me into an alcoholic. After a drink, people at bars are always more willing to have a stranger take their photos, and it's easier for me to ask too. So here we are at a bar again. While sitting there sipping away, my friend saw a large spider crawling on his murse and he gently flicked it off. Unaware of his own spider-flicking strength, he watched in horror as the spider flew three feet away, then eyed us as it dramatically died.

Overcome by guilt, we needed to relocate. As we were fleeing the crime scene, this traveling man walked by so we grabbed him. I'm calling him Spider Man, because the spider corpse is literally right behind him in this photo, and that was the happenings at the moment, so it was all I could think about. Yeah, the photo is blurry, so I'm calling it trauma-induced.

Redhead/beard count: 17

Dead spider region.

FacToid: Real spiders are not known to drink alcohol, which makes his presence here questionable.

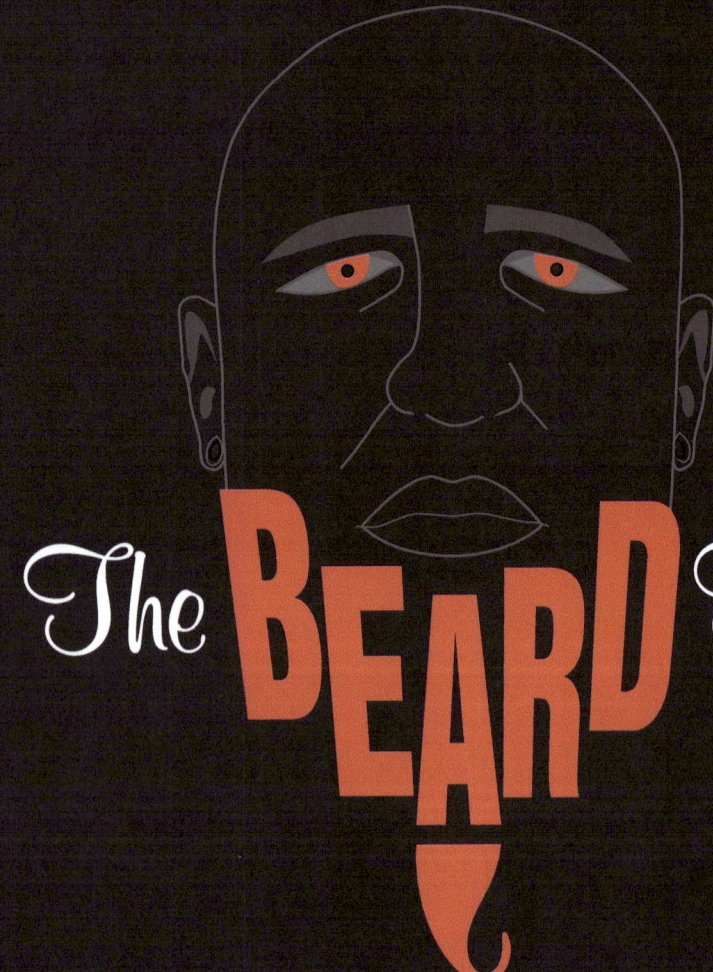

The BEARD Hunter CLUB

After getting into beard hunting, I discovered I have friends who also like hunting beards. The next few pages are a collection of their prey that I was more than happy to include in the book. They found some good'uns.

This might inspire me to carry on hunting for a while. Call me crazy, but collaborations have a way of doing that. Less work for me, and more variety for you, is not to be frowned at.

The BEARD Hunter CLUB

Photos by: Chiaki Hachisu
Hunting location: San Diego, CA

My friend Chiaki hunted this dude down. San Diego represent.

photo by Chiaki Hachisu

photo by Chiaki Hachisu

The BEARD Hunter CLUB
Photos by: Chiaki Hachisu

CHI CHI'S
Man

This is Chiaki's husband, Richie Ditta. He owns a bike repair shop, just like my other red-headed bike shop guy earlier in the book. They're about 600 miles apart, but I bet they know each other. The bike messenger world is very small.

Richie's been rockin' the flavor saver for a long time now and it always seems to be trying to reach out and touch someone.

A wisp that says "Wheeeee".

photo by Chiaki Hachisu

Redhead/beard count: 18

The BEARD Hunter CLUB

Photos by: Kevin Bergthold.
Hunting location: Denver, CO

Proud beard wearer told his friends they were not good enough to be photographed.

Fictionoid: You could drive a car through those tunnels.

photo by Kevin Bergthold

Another bike shop owner. I'm nicknaming him Wolfie.

A beard you could store your wallet in.

The BEARD Hunter CLUB
Photos by: Kevin Bergthold

Oh Hai. Vinnie bartends with Kevin's wife Jessica.

Don't be scared. It's only beer.

photos by Kevin Bergthold

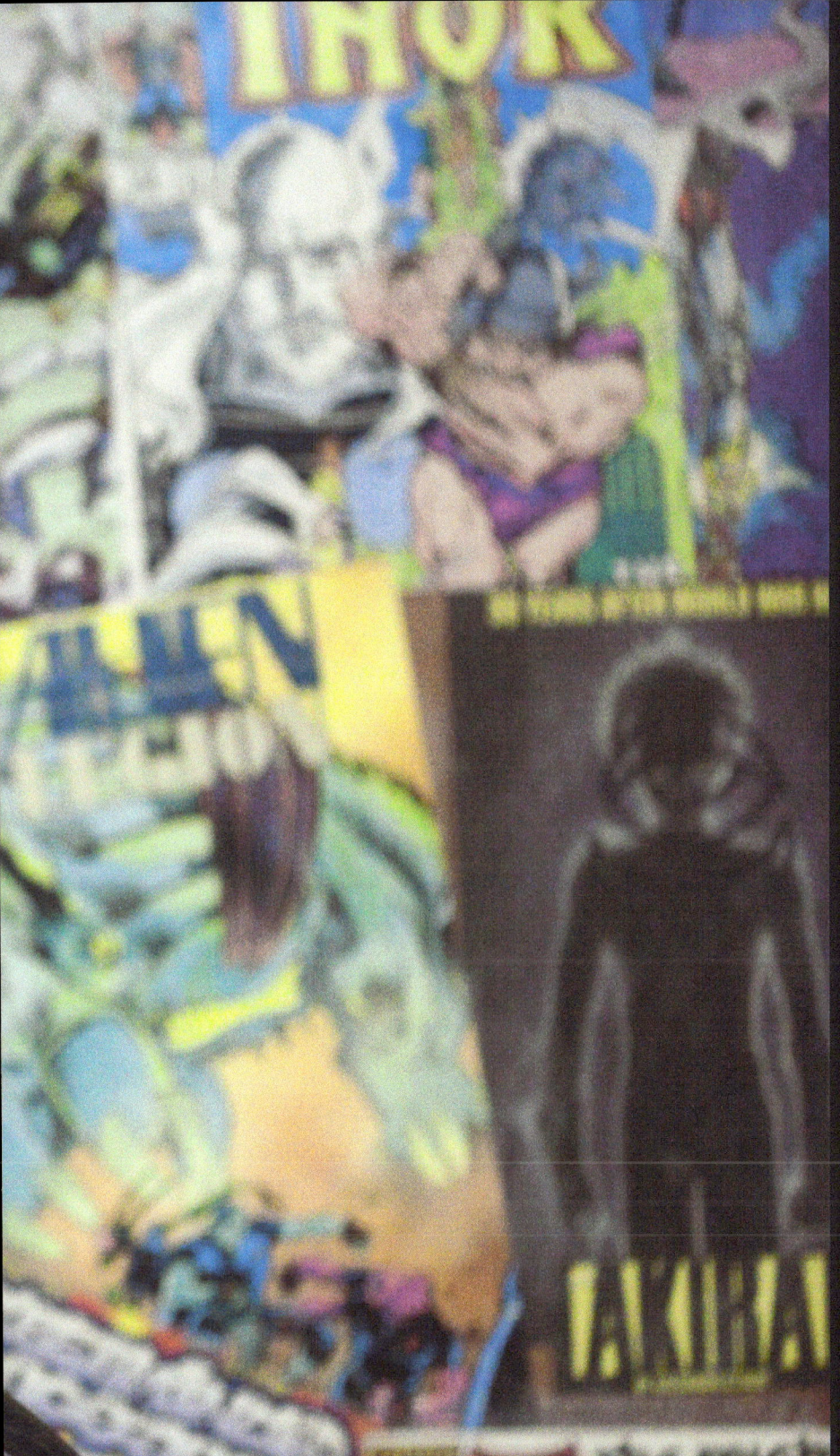

The BEARD Hunter CLUB

Photos by: Kevin Bergthold

Someone likes comic books. I'm guessing for this guy it was just a circumstantial backdrop. I'd stand there.

He plays in band called Minor Note Orchestra.

The BEARD Hunter CLUB

Photos by: Kevin Bergthold

Handlebar moustache in progress by Squidds Madden. He said he's not going to shave his beard until he's successful.

photo by Kevin Bergthold

Fresh out of the pen. He's been working on his firey beard for five years.

If you've watched the TV show "Shameless," you probably agree that this guy looks like William H. Macy's character Frank Gallagher.

photo by Kevin Bergthold

Redhead/beard count: 19

The BEARD Hunter CLUB

Photos by: Kevin Bergthold

Visiting Denver from Oklahoma and wants to relocate to Colorado for his band, a blues rock outfit.

photo by Kevin Bergthold

BACK TO
Basics

Chris is the husband of a friend of mine. I shot him cutting wood because they heat their house with a wood burning stove, and he takes pride in working so hard to provide heat for his family. He has been growing his beard for a year without trimming, and it is still pretty thin. You can't see it from the photos, but his wife makes him custom overalls, and the ones he's wearing have a giant catfish on them.

—Jason Wilkey

photo by Jason Wilkey

I think Jason's photos of this guy are hot. The only fuel and pollution from Chris doing his own wood chopping was probably some hummus and the fart that followed it.

Redhead/beard count: 20

The BEARD Hunter CLUB
Photos by: Jason Wilkey

BACK TO THE Bricks

I met Evan through a friend on Facebook. We didn't have a long shoot, but I like the main shot I got from him. He works at a local tattoo shop in my area.
—Jason Wilkey

Guess what?! More earring tunnels. I almost didn't notice due to the excellent, old school brick wall advertisement behind him. A corporation will probably paint over that soon. They seem to really enjoy destroying historical flavor.

Redhead/beard count: 21

photo by Jason Wilkey

The BEARD Hunter CLUB

Photos by: Jason Wilkey

BACK TO THE
Band

This is Matt, the boyfriend of a photographer friend of mine. He has recently learned to play the ukulele and is very good. He also plays guitar and is a beginning photographer.

—Jason Wilkey

No tunnels or red hair, but still fabulous.

I wonder if he's playing "The Rainbow Connection?"

Nice one for helping the kids, Steven! Nice eyebrows too. Where do you get them done?

The BEARD Hunter CLUB

Photos by: Jason Wilkey

BACK TO THE
Beginning

This is my cousin Steven. He can grow out a beard like this in just a few months. I shot him at the gym, because he recently found out he is borderline diabetic and needs to lose weight. So far, he's lost about 40 lbs.

He works as a caregiver at a children's home.

—Jason Wilkey

photos by Jason Wilkey

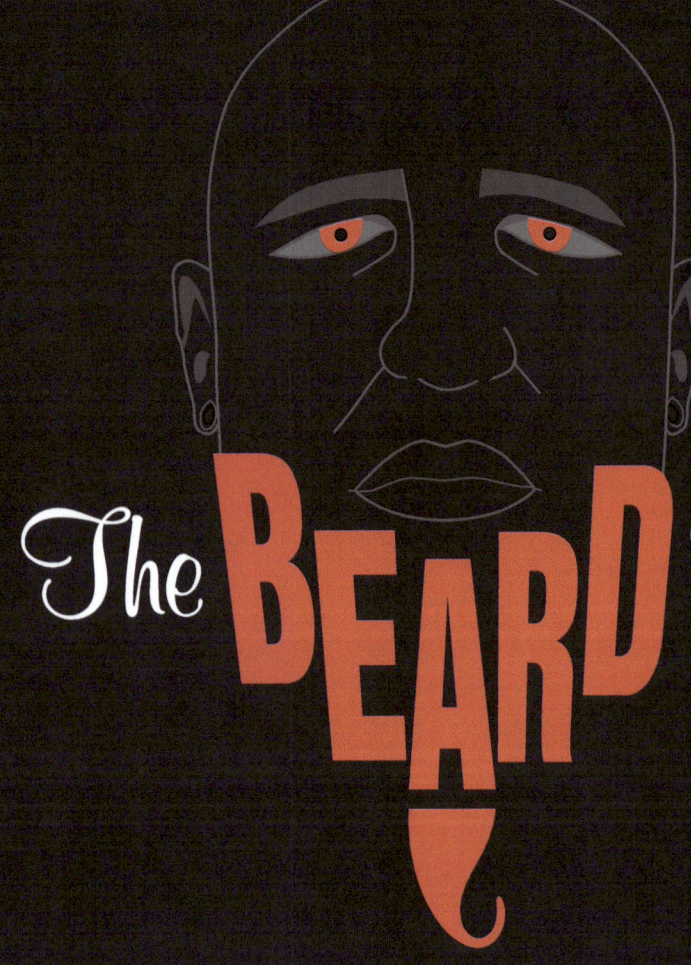

The BEARD Hunter FALSIES

Beards are everywhere, not just on people's faces. For fun, here's a little collection of the not-so-real kind.

La Fée VERTE

Feeling particularly artsy, I decided to include my Cappiello poster, found in my living room. Easy hunt. This poster is of "The Green Fairy," which is also a nickname for absinthe.

My reflection might look like I'm waving to you, but what I'm really doing is going for the absinthe bottle. After all, it was a long week, and I told you this book was going to make me an alcoholic!

The fact that this fairy doesn't have toes continues to bother me every time I look at this poster.

129

The BEARD Hunter FALSIES

MISSION Drive BY

Here we have a drive-by of the right kind. No one was hurt and my subject didn't have to sign a photo release. Win-win. This section of a mural with a crazy, bearded bloke is in the Mission District neighborhood of San Francisco, where the streets are full of beautiful murals.

The oTher Blue Beard. He mighT have a parroT Tucked somewhere, buT a piraTe he is noT. →

The BEARD Hunter FALSIES

I think he likes his b'day cake.

YOU HAVE A LITTLE *Face* ON YOUR ICING

Of the many things I like to do, here are two of them in one: hunt and bake. This was a b'day cake for my honey. That was one tasty beard. I don't make a habit of eating beards, but this was the exception. It's also the only purple beard I've found on my hunts. If I had done this project in the 90s, I would have found a rainbow of beard colors.

Redhead/beard count: 22

BEARDED *Beak*   A.K.A. — The Bone Crusher.

Say hello to my old friend ... Bobbie. She flies around my house and tries to eat everyone's food. This time she succeeded and formed this food beard from a soyrizo casserole dish that was very tasty. This would take a human at least half an hour to develop, but she was able to make it in less than two minutes. Also note her beard matches her eyes. What a hipster.

Although I shouldn't, I have to say the kernels of corn in her beard remind me of some of the homeless guys I've seen wandering around the city yelling gibberish at the pedestrians. A real stomach turner.

BEARD Hunter FALSIES

FacToid: Using gliTTer on arT projecTs always resulTs in several flakes of gliTTer sTuck To your face for aT leasT four hours, unTil someone graciously poinTs iT ouT.

LIL' Nutter

Introducing "Peanut Butter," created by my friend Adam's son, Desi, just for this project. Desi's birthday is coming up in September, and if his dad will let me, I'd like to buy him a puppy. He easily earned it. How cute is that gold-bearded smiley face?

No herbal ecsTasy was required To execuTe This drawing, even Though iT may appear ThaT iT was.

Art-CHIVES

I found this one in with a bunch of old drawings I did over a decade ago. Meet a guy I knew in Los Angeles who made herbal ecstasy and rarely left his home. His house had almost no furniture and he couldn't have cared less. He was completely insane and somewhat scary, but high enough that you knew he wouldn't kill you if you had glow sticks on you. Needless to say, the friendship lasted that proverbial New York minute.

The BEARD Hunter FALSIES

Tarred and feathered Thumb results.

OLD TOM *Thumb*

My book, my rules. Beards come in all forms, right? Well, this is what happens when I get turned down by a bearded prospect twice in one day. It's either do something like this or quietly ball up in a corner and rock. This seemed more fun to me, and more productive.

My lil bearded thumb puppet is made with bird feathers from the "Bearded Beak" bird you saw a few pages back. Tom Thumb came to exist out of the little feather fuzzies the parrot left all over the house, so I did some recycling and voilà!

Theory: This Santa suit is probably still being used at a mall and most likely has never been cleaned.

Although yellow and brown leisure suits are hot, they sadly never came back in style.

Disco SANTA

I did a little hunting through my old photos and POOF: Santa beard with a mini me on his lap.

What was my mother thinking when she dressed me that day? I look like a giant, aging banana. The 70s ... says it all.

Somebody needs To give This caT a TooThbrush.

NICE *Kitty?*

Do cats have beards? Do they have tattoos? This one does, but it's not real. Shhhhhh. What is it, you ask? It's the Cheshire Cat representation from the videogame *American McGee's Alice*. The man-doll version.

I AM THE WI-FI *Overlord*

Wireless is a must these days, and I share mine with my immediate neighbors, who don't want to hassle with getting their own.

This is the contribution envelope from one of the neighbor friends. I'm on the computer so much that if I had a beard, it would probably look just like that.

ABOUT THE AUTHOR

Me

Daily Prey

BFF Jennifer. She had no idea at the time, but in this photo her hair is filling in as the beard I'm unable to grow due to my lethal supply of estrogen.

Juliann Brown

Talking about myself isn't my favorite thing, so I'll keep this brief. I grew up in the sticks of Southern Illinois, where I was surrounded by a lot of hunting and fishing. I was never a fan of either sport, or the results of them, so I feel hunting for beards is a great twist on what is embedded in my memory, and my soul, from that childhood. In 1988, I moved to San Diego and pursued an education and career in graphic design. Over the years, I worked my way up the coast, and San Francisco has been my stomping grounds since 2000. Although my career has been fruitful, I finally decided to break away from the man to do my own thing, this book. I hope to bring you more in the future!

That's a wrap!